AIR FOR SLEEPING FISH

GILLIAN FERGUSON

Air for
Sleeping Fish

BLOODAXE BOOKS

ISBN: 1 85224 416 X

First published 1997 by
Bloodaxe Books Ltd,
P.O. Box 1SN,
Newcastle upon Tyne NE99 1SN.

Bloodaxe Books Ltd acknowledges
the financial assistance of Northern Arts.

Cover printing by J. Thomson Colour Printers Ltd, Glasgow.

Printed in Great Britain by
Cromwell Press Ltd, Broughton Gifford, Melksham, Wiltshire.

to JAMES MURRAY FERGUSON
and MOIRA FERGUSON,
my mother and father,
for their love and belief

Acknowledgements

Three of these poems were first published in Maura Dooley's anthology *Making for Planet Alice* (Bloodaxe Books, 1997). Acknowledgements are due to the editors of the following publications in which some of the others first appeared: *Chapman, Scotland on Sunday,* and *A Tribute to Norman MacCaig* (Chapman Publications, 1995).

I would also like to express extreme gratitude to the Scottish Arts Council for a Writer's Bursary awarded in 1993.

Contents

Winter Walk

Under a white skin of ice,
the river's clear veins push
air for sleeping fish.

Sun shatters on the hills'
blue spines, showers snow
with flashing dust.

In a dribbling cave we find
stone's slow tears
have made organ pipes of icicles,

a graveyard of unicorns.
You unroof two fluted horns
for your leaf-eyed head,

dance under armed trees.
I gather petticoats of starched web,
a blood-crown of cut haws.

Through many wind-shaped drifts
I hold your glove-furred paw
until air and fields blush.

Blue-breathed creatures let us stay
under these dragoned clouds
as birds' hearts flutter into silence,

the bloomed dusk falls,
under the knife of night;
the cold fires of space spark –

frozen in our own myth
with the moon veining our wooded path,
printing our feet with wildcat and deer.

Bad News

A grey dog of sky
curls in the horizon,
snarling and pawing
the small ball of sun.

Hills – stone crowns snow-blown –
lace their white shawls
into wind-twitched sands
of unmollusced mother of pearl.

Seconds puffed like cold birds,
growing into frozen hours,
night-hued, bloated,
as bad news ruined my blood,

splitting the veins in seamless skin,
bursting my drum heart –
an overblown rose
drowning petals in the sea.

You have leapt from love
like a salmon, forever
in your element of air,
slipped from my liquid hands.

Manacled to time,
I crush my watch shell
but light still dies
on the gory water slab.

I lift a curlew's slim bones
and authored skull –
the beak at my lips
accurately shapes sound.

Winter Sunflowers

You cradle mouthless smiling flowers
through sparkled streets, bending winds,
yellow heads heavy in your crooked arm –
haloes in the grope of twilight.

Earth fish, summer snow, winter sunflowers –
an impossible gift races your heart home;
a torch to France's burning fields,
armies of flowers in rooted rows –

tournesols craning laden green sinews,
straining sky and eye to be more blue.
The sure colour of a child's sun
has sparked your January eyes,

a spring in their leaf shades
that thirsty summer crisped;
the seeds of grinning health.
Bold black single eyes

are laughing in their fat-petalled skirts
at thin lilies in serious moon-white gowns –
we hold solar blooms like cheerleaders.
Staked by our own two skeletons

we stand watered in the winter
eclipse of the dark days fallen –
born in the blind earth of life
love grows us like light.

Butterfly Kisses

After a warm afternoon of nectar,
flowers giving him the eye –
'Come sup at my perfumed cup;
I the most open, soft-lipped, sweetest' –

a red admiral staggering in air
like a street drunk groping invisible walls,
tipped his sail-big wing on my lashes.
I have that smiling spine at the touch of any kind wild thing,

and now too the smiling thought,
this was the real thing, a butterfly kiss,
imitations so often feathered on my giggling cheek,
fairy lights in the blue sky of my father's eye;

years after by my lover's lady-sickening, sooty camel fringes,
among the first new toys since childhood's soft gang.
I knew then he would continue what delighted
my father's child; his dead mother's favourite kiss.

Dear Norman

(for the late Norman MacCaig)

I blew in from my own young night
and demented Edinburgh November,
magnetised leaves tangled in Ophelia hair.

Whisky soon lay like a cat
on my stomach – its water, like you,
ran briskly forty years ago;

each year we celebrated with a Silk Cut –
mist peered at our lung-blown rival,
a dovetail of poems fanned in your hand.

How your chameleon mind, frail giant,
whose words skewer fragments of the world –
butterflies in boxes of books –

alchemised the blades of wit
to feathers. Your wife dead;
our pain surpassing all soberness.

Your hieroglyphs translated my pages,
laughter poulticed dry tears;
words summed like scars on stone.

Your tongue still speaks like light
in black holes of belief –
I remember my homeward, hovercraft feet.

The Swimming Pool Ghost

In splintering shallows at the local pool,
a ghost shifts – a shoal of pink minnows
that never comes up for air again.

A terminal dive into three feet of thin water.
Corrugated spine. Skull grenade.

Climbing from the slow skin
of emptied indoor water,
a goggled woman scoured
her shocked body raw.

You can mistake him for the breathless lengths
of underwater swimmers, but pass clean through –
a touch of cold current as he disperses.

No mermaids here.
No scenic carcasses of sunken ships.
Nothing of how my friend saw his death
as he drowned in a beautiful place:
a Mexican bay in the evening
like a basin of blood.

Water slapped kisses on his lips,
a mute choir of fancy-coloured fish
mouthing in the waves –
lungs could breathe water
like the living sponge.

The swimming pool ghost
ripples around children –
churning cherubs with plastic wings –
because there was no time
to make tableaux of his death,
for mouths cushioning bedside air
with comfortable words.

Because he died in the wrong metaphor
like a baby dropped in a font.

Because sudden death is crime
against the spirit, he waits
at the scene for a just court.

When the pool is drained,
will he swim in air
like a wingless salmon,

or rush to the sluice –
to dive, be swallowed
by bottomless sea.

Small Town

Chimneys breathe slow webs;
they hitch on moving air.

The moon scatters black roofs
with shifting fish-scales,

glasses eyes
on fur-footed shadows.

I shake the city
like a wet dog –

another silent midnight
soothing as temporary death

where the same names
breed on stones.

First Visit to Your Mother's Grave

(for Richard)

Cradled in cloud,
the sun still makes snow
weep down the hill's stone face.
Your eyes are lost in tiger lilies.

Will grief swallow you
as earth swallows stones
ruined by wind,
digested by rain?

*

Your boy is here, hand in hand.
Can you see through these daisy eyes,
focused in this particular air
or soil like a scent, a silence?

Or can I bring you down to him,
touch this stone like a lightning rod?
Or do we always walk in trinity
with the patient love of the dead.

*

I swear to Mary your mother,
on the gold scars of her name,
to be there among the living,
to lift the baton of care,

and turning from the barred gate,
see the black stone melt
in the twilight flames
of flowers left behind.

The Lion Summer

Lost in a lion summer –
sweating flowers' sweet reek,
the iris sky's blinding white pupil,

you floated back to winter
snowflake-frail – a word's
shaped breath wounding;

a diagram of bones,
sail clothes scooped by wind –
eyes dull as iced puddles.

I soothe, cover,
with my bandage of skin;
my cool fingers

pavement roots
probing ears and lids,
the smooth hood of skull.

Acute angles all night
my soft earth moulds,
and in the longer day

each garden tear
sprouts another snowdrop
like the white crosses of the Somme.

Fear of the Future

Around flowers,
the sun draws coloured haloes;
sainted, green-haired earth –
a minefield in pastoral disguise.

Yawning air does not fool me –
explosions lurk,
will rip its throat
like hounds on deer and fox.

I bruise petals
with my heavy sole,
smell their blood –
I even fear butterflies

might fall and shatter
like kaleidoscopes.
My breath is tiny pieces of wind –
I know the rabbit's paralysis.

Clothes Moths

Cotton, cashmere, lambswool
noticed holed; sieved silk –
a growing home mystery,

until a small moth
the colour of past things –
Victorian ivory, tissued veils

in shilling-scribbled boxes,
wedding menus of dead brides,
twinkled through the room.

Then more, sailing radiator air
from the cupboard harbour of clothes.

I thought moths a problem long gone
like the scent of lavender on linen,
Eau-de-cologne; scoured

the city for camphor balls,
naphthalene. But night light
still snowed hordes

on sliver-of-bone, talcumed wings;
they rose silently from duvets, drawers,
waiting winter coats, jacket-shouldered chairs

until I was spooked –
an incurable plague, small but biblical,
to make us humble, naked as animals;

ghosts of the future come
with dust in their blind white eyes
to warn of worm, insect, and digesting soil;

until you clapped
another slow clothes moth
to death;

'See,' you said –
'killed by a high fibre diet!'

Stags in Glen Clova

Russet caught in dull flames
of dying fern;

living trophies hung
on the sky's gold wall,

sharing black designs
with windless trees –

even the heart of tough earth,
heather-sinewed,

thuds at their coming hooves.
All day I hunt them

for my heart,
to store wildness there

like heather's sweet tongues
in honey jars.

But I stumble
into stony dusk,

night's skinning wind –
shrink in my bald bones

at stags sudden rising
close to my hornless head.

Honeymoon in St Lucia

See beloved —

how white flowers
powder night air
with pollen —

ghosts breathing
gold dust and perfume
from their lungs;

the moon hung low
to be our lamp;
the insistent stream

drowning its voice
in a silver pool.
Fetch the grape's

eldest blood
to stain our lips;
stir those birds

with cobalt fire
in their crests
and sweet voices,

for nothing
will cross
our stars.

See beloved —

how old tongues
waken in our mouths,
how ritual has left
the church in us —

our eyes flood the world,
day and night twin temples
wherein we rejoice.

Everything is sacred.

       *

Luxurious in St Lucia,
anointed with oil,
cloud nudges
the advertised sun –

drops pock
the blue pool,
fill the throats of flowers,
speckle stone lizards.

But sunlight survives,
fire and water at once –
as our love still shone
in a year of nights.

       *

These white-mooned nights –
your sleeping skin shines,
impossible and brilliant
as fireflies sprinkled in the trees.

End of the Year

Weeping yellow leaves,
the pond willow shelters

its drowned twin.
Skeletons of honesty shake

brittle moon membranes.
Last flowers cower

at the north wind's slap;
the sky gloved in grey.

Before winter's critical light,
I shed a layer

of my growing self.
Shaped as a snake's skin,

my ghosts haunt
every instant of the past,

unconscious
of the windowed present;

moving their lips and hands
in endless words and gestures.

Weak

Wind a handless sculptor
rounding hips and breast,
automatic air in me,
hold me up –

I am caught
by the skirt of tough flowers
at the wading mountain's knee.

I Do Not Cry Like I Used To

I do not cry like I used to,
I think like my granny talking dancing.

These boulders fell in my river bed,
dried me up in case I drowned.

But blind water
forced rivulets through bad American films,

soaps and injured animals.
The News.

Then see my mascara railroad,
my happy white hanky.

I surrender; the boulders tremble,
threaten to roll.

The Handprint

A white shadow loomed
on my first sautéd skin –

I thought a palm leaf's
fingered shade

had patterned me
spread on sand.

But sun beat copper
in my arm's pink fire –

a handprint was there,
sharp as splashed bleach.

And I thought of the perfect stranger
dragging me safe

from the crazed car
hunting the island road –

his blinding smile;
halo of hair.

In Hospital-land

A virus nibbled the delicacy of my father's brain.
Nonsense streamed from his cracked lips,
hitching a ride on galloping grammar –

the kind in the book I feared so much
I weighted it nightly with my heaviest toys
in case the pictures squeezed out into my dreams –

a man-sized rabbit with red-jelly eyes
whose words jitter me still when late and wired,
and her, blonde and banded just like me

holding a baby which turned to a pig
as under my hands now you might turn to a corpse –
why was there no blood from such unusual violence?

The delicate curve of long flamingo necks
beating terrified hedgehog spikes –
a voice saying, *'Off with his head'* as the only solution.

I ran down a corridor horribly bright
as if my screams might call you back
from checking out rumours of irresistible light,

and when I was so small I looked at feet,
a hand held out a glass of water,
a gesture as plain as a label saying DRINK ME.

Why did she take the poisonous potion?
Why didn't she just shout DADDY
who would make it all stop?

Slugs

Without the decency of shells,
slugs reveal themselves
on the steps suddenly lit.

Uniform brown,
the slow armourless army
advances in silent night manoevres.

Bodies seethe,
dumb but wounded
by light melting on the move.

A mucous map
smears the stones;
the route of some repulsive purpose –

but blind
they do not stumble,
one long belly

can go no lower;
all obstacles
patiently assailed.

Connoisseurs of air,
horns tremble
at exquisite samples –

the breath of flowers,
leaf-stir,
sun-burned soil.

The moon transfigures
slime – they bleed
original silver

as crude worms
spin silk.
Like a life trail

viscid with sin
polished
by God.

Reclaiming the Garden

The gardener long dead,
his dog bones,

weeds are hysterical;
jaundiced roses, scrawny-shanked,

sugar summer air;
the old tree is goitred

by a murderous
honeysuckle embrace.

Basement moles,
we surface to labour

until air and blood
christen black soil –

we set tame green fires
to burn this wasteland down.

Morning Now

My spine ridge gleams
with the juice of kisses –

rounded like the sea's
insistent licking

of sharp rocks.
This is morning now –

from the shipwrecked light
to knowledge that home

is in you like blood,
around you like skin:

the world's salt taste
overcome by your tongue.

Comforters

(for Nan Spowart)

Evening bruises the sky
until black,
pitted with stars.

No grave sleep
loosens my bones.

He is not dead,
no longer dying,
but will forever
only haunt himself
like the shell grieving
its pearl — a seed
its withered flower.

A skin of silence
seals air —
broken by the alchemy
of guts, it closes
on me like a wound.

Crisis cannot be long,
days hustled into weeks —
I know your mouths and hands
but lips, fingers fail.

Like blood-bats satisfied,
your voices deafen only air.

Like this blind moon
you have all turned into shadow.

All except you,
startling my heart
with sudden calls —

words warm like arms
until I see the violet promise
of morning's blue complexion
in the sky –

flawed only
by the first loud birds.

Dependent

All foundations slide.
Time stretches its snake spine –

huts, hovels folding silently
in ageing landscapes,

but towers too, sunburnt spires;
monumental seed bodies.

Clouds close on vacant air,
a storm in earth like dense sea –

dust rises
in a slow blindness over light.

And who can ever bandage me
with words?

Are these survivors
in a firefly swarm

picking the dark ruins
for golden straws

in crude rubble;
primitive bricks?

Love in Season

Summer.
Haze like a breathable drug –
Rouen miming a dream.

From its white throat,
the square fountain spat
diamonds in our hair.

In the cathedral,
thin spire a cat's needle claw
scratching the sky
to open like a door to heaven,
I understood haloes.

Cousins of light,
love intense enough to see;
an explosion from the heart
too full of loud muscle,
violent blood.

Wings –
the bloom of spirit
sailing its burden
towards the light.

Winter.
My skin is rimmed
with absence.

Anger burns the blueprint
of a perfect life unlived,
but pure sorrow
turns itself holy.

Your snow of letters
melted on the mat
and no spring came.

The Owl's Hour

Break, break in the owl's hour –
slow blood slugging the heart,
blue veins written
on night-white skin.

The moon, trawled into a crow's nest,
tangles window light
on juiced eyes,
alone hands paired.

Break, break before dumb skies,
crowded with the deaths of stars,
to know life blind,
but spits and smiles.

Love at Easter

All that Good Friday,
tears of saints fell;
trees wept long icicles.

Impervious as eskimos,
we pocked the smooth complexion
of the hill –

white,
rounded as a skull.
Printed ourselves.

Simple fire in your blood
ignited skin
like torchlight

suffocated by a hand –
I was melted
from long frost.

Arms eagled for joy
in low sun's slow gold,
we made blue crucifix shadows –

the day of death,
two died – one rose:
invincible.

Arum Lilies

My eyes dive
into poreless white lilies
open as a lover,

to powder my tongue
with arum sperm
like yellow sherbert.

For silent-throated mouths
my lips now speak –
coldness and light

transparent in petal skin;
sucking veins
in my heart's clear blood.

I wind a crown
of bible flowers
with the fast life of snow –

lizard-skin ghosts
belled in moonlight,
sounding to dust

in the dance
for the death of your fire –
its licking flames and black touch.

First Flat

Crackled bone sinks,
snake-mottled chrome,
crumbling curtains of rosy chenille;

Victorian garlands of soot,
mirrors for vampires,
linoleum and lead.

Newspapers, jaundiced,
break news of the second war
to the fire's dead heart.

Blood on my fingers,
I christen my home with sweat,
strip her cold cocoon,

lay bare its wooden skeleton,
thread bright arterial wires;
paint the colour of warm skin.

I lie in the outlined space
where she died –
doors scarred by violent entry,

but darkness has no hands,
no breath to bowl
soft nests of dust.

But still I fear –
only one Christmas card and red bills
miss her.

Seeing

Your angel wears
such heavy disguise –
two faces,
voice of a snake.

I knew a man so good,
you saw his angel
draped around him
like a drunken friend.

Adrift from bodies,
flocks of dead
folded in air.

Animals extinct
print hurt earth
with silent feet.

I touch blind stones
to learn peace
from slow decay –

feel twin magnets
of darkness
and light.

Where Are You?

Where are you now?

In which space the air you breathe –
samples outside, where wind
shepherds sheep-clouds
seamlessly patchworked
over vast distance.

Where are you now?

I hear myself in earless silence –
your photograph drowned
in my eyes;
my ribs sharpen
like a sucking cage.

Where are you now?

Around me, a globe of absence grows –
stars wink knowingly
when night rolls in;
you are everywhere
I am not.

Night Map

Bandaged by darkness,
my eyes open a night map,

black with contusions of ink blue
around luminous points,

silver-threaded —
like membraned prints

of ancient heavens.
Each point a person loved,

who loves me,
an axis to plot myself.

Those I can find
with bat senses,

hang for a moment
above their beds

to fingerlessly touch —
like unknown kisses

planted on a child's
dreamy forehead.

Twin

I want to be
your Siamese twin –

lying this near
so long,

fooled skin
might close distance,

thin as paper,
like a wound.

Then death
will not divide us.

But your sleeping eyes flutter
in a cage of dreams;

no vein map leads
to love's source –

in one body
still other,

even with hearts
a double yolk.

Light and the Year

Light and the year are dying.
Light decays, a veil of rotten silk
hung each day thinner on the winter sky,
still soiled by darkness.

The past draws harder at the year,
we clutch at months, grasp only hours,
crumbling into seconds;
and blinded by the lounging dusks

fumble in the dust for fallen dreams.
But smug with a million springs,
insured by seeds, the earth turns
silently away —

and long nights telescoping days
threaten to collide
in a slow blink like death
broadening its black margins.

Cliff House, Orkney Isles

Stone has rounded
on your limpet home,
house, cliff
becoming one.

And I envied your life –
daily sighs
as the wide lip
of spent water

mouths pearl sands;
evening suns bleeding
on broken mirrors
of sea.

But light turning
gulls to angels
suffocates in cloud;
wind that kneels

this crippled tree,
hanging hope in berry clots,
hunts darkness
squatting at your window.

And on long winter nights,
drowned sailors' cries;
lonely men laughing
under landless stars.

Outdoor Artist

Leaves boil
in a hunting wind;

fields spattered
with wild flowers –

a fierce sun rages
from a cage of clouds.

Bruised vermilion and blue,
rusted brown,

burned charcoal black,
his hands are weary

for their essences.
The fruit of days

they lie spoiled
on the canvas –

brilliant
in their cloaks of paint.

Each Man Is an Island

Skin the hours
that separate forever
the lights of the world
in a cyclops sky –

moon eye silver-lidded
like a sleeping snake;
staring sun eye
lashed with flames.

Symmetrical hearts
promise unity
as darkness slithers
into air still bloodied

by the dying sun.
But love's smile
is two-faced, four-lipped
as Janus.

Autumn Seat

The green pulse stilled,
leaf sets leaf
with slow flames.

Shadow-trees
inch over blades
of silver grass.

Futures coil
like secret flowers
in fallen seed –

the ripe sun
touching my eyes
with golden blindness.

Signals

Once in the mad topography of love
ruled by two giants,
I could find you anywhere –

our breathing heard in the sea,
our curved bodies the lounging hills,
sun and moon our eyes.

We were the world.
Then storm, tremor, eclipse.
I called and called

like the inconsolable gulls –
only white noise
breaking into silence.

Grey Kirk in the Mearns

Perched, a stained skull
on an ancient skeleton
of wind-picked hill,

the grey kirk
clutches veils of sleet
about its scoured bone.

Glazed sockets
spill no colour
on melting snow.

Once fleshed
with bodies broken
on this brutal soil,

it was the head
of its cold religion.
Empty,

it still wears the frown
of dour old ministers
set in stone.

Over-fishing

Picked by winter's fingers
like table chickens –
razor-bills, guillemots, little auks.

Wind pleads their wings,
missing the raucous angels fallen
from the rough heaven of Scottish sky.

From the choking sea,
waves cough more and
more corpses on the shore –

fish shunted
from the jaws of ships.
Wrong or rare.

Only light lives,
tickling
their silver sides.

Grief

Like those shoots I found
feeding on the cupboard dark,

grief swallows despair,
drinks tears,

to seed
in my circular blood.

Opium Poet

The black blood of poppies
darkens your veins.

Night unfolds
its blinding cloths –

the moon a hole
cut into heaven.

Stars sing
with slow silver tongues

songs that never end.
Owl and mouse move.

From trees you gather
words like leaves

until dawn shivers
in the sky –

your pen dips
into a mind

open as a page.
Open to the world

beneath the veil
of stone, soil, skin.

Perpetual Winter

Prising six ruby hearts
from the pomegranate's bloody comb,

she burst them with guilt on her palate,
until her mouth ran like a wound –

six months of shackled light;
seeds the prison of riotous flowers.

           *

Her network of night creatures
the blind moon's mercury eyes;
mirrors of loch;

sea her moving skirt,
hemmed with sequinned spume,
seamed to her black bodice of air,

dragged nightly
on a hairless progress
attended by stars.

The ancient gown defiled,
her pocked face turns
empty of warmth

as drained veins –
frost grips earth
like a crocodile.

War in the Gulf

Human sounds in trees'
bending spines;
fingered branches claw
night's black fabric
tented over earth,
to lay bare
a bone-coloured moon.

Widows dig
for memories –
compare the war
that spawned film,
to one swallowing it live.

There is no right
or wrong any more –
only people,
plumbed with blood,
cocooned in whole skins,
fearing sleep
in treeless sands.

The Winter Rose

(for Dr James Hawkins)

Blue-handed, with difficult string,
I staked the broken winter rose,

unbending fibres of green spine,
lifting a crumpled white face –

rain-teared, blinded with earth;
finished by axing winds.

So many thorns hid in the leaves,
and light so thin,

my task lasted even as snow
rehearsed Christmas in the garden.

And when I would have drowned
in snow, an angel came –
I had no words or gold.

But I saw the crushed bush
ghosted with buds;

her face now upturned – furred,
snug in snow – to stars;

after sleeping summer
ironing new petals with air.

And when I would have drowned
in snow, an angel came –
I had no words or gold.

Seal Virus

Seals come —

sun-dimpled,
not creasing water
ironed by evening.

Eyes so large,
sailors dived in
and never came back;

where light writes
with blood draining
from a wounded cloud —

so many dead white children.
Our stone eyes
return to the stream,

so silently, seals go.

The Day You Stopped Calling Me Darling

Your hand shone my shoulders'
flesh-padded blades –
the nubs of love's wings.

Keen as the holy prince
my name slipped
into its common disguise,

then drowned
like a spider on the page –
anteater eager

I hoovered your speech,
heard only its rattle,
hard as tacks.

The world groans
with huge sorrows,
but scale is nothing
to the hurt heart
where words carve
absences like knives.

I must swallow
my fine feelings –
come down to earth,

grounded
like a moth
glutted on silk.

Back to the Hills

Out in pouncing rain
and sun when clouds crack
open like a smile

again; tough feathers,
soft-wire stems of bracken
high as my eye

until silver birch
lift shining thigh bones
out of bell heather.

From hill's root
to eagle air,
spot fires of rowan,

inhabiting my skin
in bouldered steps,
her without words

or age, sucking wind,
arms stag-branched;
heart on the moon.

Flower Power

Agitator spring
hangs blueprints –
braille in air –
for each blind seed.

Underground activists,
their purpose spreads –
slow green fire
whispering over earth,

until strident stalks
shout at eyes –
unclenching fists
of colour to the sun.

Rowan Trees

Heather swarms purple over hills,
green crooks of fern ending in fire;
flames of red deer running.

Colour startles my eye
from the mind's black cloths,
insisting –

and these trees,
their thickness of leaves
armour against evil,

showing heaven's blood
in bullet holes of berries
spotting the dusk veil.

Unrequited

If the heart is more
than blood in veins
pumping muscle,
furring and failing,
you are there.
Caught in the idea:

a bird at a window.

Silent as Roses

When there is too much to say
then we are silent –
silent as roses

whose red hearts
shout love
above the blood-drawing thorn.

Our stiff lips a dam,
tongues drown,
wet lashes excruciate.

As sea speaks to crushed shells,
sun to clouds it burns,
moon to dying stars,

we fill
day and night
with our silence.

Winter Flight to Thailand

A claw of golden spires punctured the sun –
molten light blinded me.

I stumbled into thinning darkness,
pyramids of oranges loomed,

opening flesh of leggy lotus flowers,
golden buddhas smiling in rows.

Drugged with incense,
air was in a dream.

I flew far from your vampire tubes,
needle marks like the fast kiss of snakes;

here are the starred fingers of slow dancers,
shameless orchids tonguing warm air,

bleeding poppies; black-eyed
women rained with silver discs.

I am scoured by salt winds,
coarse birds sing in my throat.

I am grey stone, drizzle, chaotic sea;
the shivering flanks of mountains

stripped of trees.
I am history in my old blood;

frosted earth nursing tough seed,
mist kissing the rough face of scree.

I have left the land where spirit is lost
in the body's dense disguise;

here it lives open
as the walking hunger;

numbs itself in winter heat
far from your sheets of snow.

Cleared for Sheep

Wine-time in thinning gold air,
on our wobbly canvas chairs
in the country. Before moths.
Before night's colourless breath –

already the hills' bald red shins
soothing into watercolour layers,
losing their stone selves;
grass ghosting in the fields.

Our white wine rubied
by the last sliding light,
we sip its shining and follow
the simple matters of grubby sheep

pinked as roses –
the unreasonable panic of lambs;
such scales of throaty clamour,
such wriggling reunions.

Then sheep bodies bobbing
in dusk's grey flood – white surviving too
in our bodiless face and hands,
a voice travels in the real tongue –

we are hunting the fern
with electrified heart and hair
for the impossible shepherd,
his question-mark, nursery-rhyme crook.

But our eyes blur
like this day-blue sky's springing rain;
though ignorant of the music
we know a lament,

and the voice only comes
from the mouth of a sheep
tearing up roots, mild,
in the ruined square of stones.

Sunny Evening

The slow blink of my waist-thick gilded lashes
like the soft clash of lazy gates,

I watch gold slabs of phantom window
sliding down the wall –

the white ceiling blushes
like a red-haired girl.

Shining as Tutankhamun,
sleeping straight as an effigy,

your breath dizzies
galaxies of dust –

under petal shades,
I know your eyes

are charging
with love.

Sound is not particular,
summer people speak like bees;

the late light thick as water
drowning the day into silence –

I am happy,
I am happy.